Review Incentive Ideas: Boosting Positive Feedback for Your Business

Ayman Shalaby

Copyright-©-2024-Virtapress.-All-Rights-Reserved.

"No part of this publication may be reproduced, distributed, or transmitted in any form or by any means, including photocopying, recording, or other electronic or mechanical methods, or by any information storage and retrieval system without the prior written permission of the publisher, except in the case of very brief quotations embodied in critical reviews and certain other noncommercial uses permitted by copyright law."

Table of Contents

Introduction 1

Chapter 1: Understanding Customer Motivation 4

Chapter 2: Creating Effective Incentive Programs 9

Chapter 3: Gamification Techniques 15

Chapter 4: Social Media and Online Presence 22

Chapter 5: Exclusive Offers and Discounts 30

Chapter 6: Loyalty Programs and Rewards 36

Chapter 7: Personalized Experiences 42

Chapter 8: Contests and Giveaways 48

Chapter 9: Collaborative Incentives 55

Chapter 10: Technology and Automation 62

Conclusion: Implementing Your Review Incentive Programs 68

Resources 74

Introduction

In today's digital age, customer reviews have become a cornerstone of business success. They are the virtual word-of-mouth that potential customers trust when making purchasing decisions. Positive reviews can significantly boost your credibility, attract new customers, and ultimately drive sales. But how do you encourage your customers to leave those glowing reviews?

This book is designed to help you unlock the secrets of effective review incentives. Whether you're a small business owner, a marketer, or a customer service professional, you'll find actionable insights and creative ideas to inspire your customers to share their positive experiences.

We'll begin by exploring the psychology behind why customers leave reviews and what motivates them to share their feedback. Understanding these factors will help you design incentive programs that resonate with your audience.

Next, we'll delve into various incentive strategies, from gamification and social media campaigns to personalized offers and collaborative promotions. Each chapter will provide practical examples, step-by-step guides, and tips to ensure your incentive programs are both effective and ethical.

By the end of this book, you'll have a comprehensive toolkit of ideas and strategies to boost the number of positive reviews for your business. You'll learn how to create meaningful incentives that not only encourage reviews but also enhance customer loyalty and satisfaction.

So, let's get started on this journey to harness the power of positive reviews and take your business to new heights!

Chapter 1: Understanding Customer Motivation

The Psychology Behind Leaving Reviews

Customer reviews are more than just feedback—they are expressions of customer experiences, emotions, and perceptions. Understanding the psychological factors that drive customers to leave reviews is the first step in designing effective incentive programs.

1. **The Need for Recognition**: Customers often leave reviews because they want to be heard and acknowledged. Positive reviews are a way for customers to share their satisfaction and be recognized for their good judgment. Similarly, negative reviews can be a call for attention to unresolved issues.

2. **Social Proof**: People are influenced by the actions of others. When customers leave reviews, they contribute to the collective opinion that shapes the perceptions of future customers. This sense of contributing to a community or helping others make informed decisions is a powerful motivator.

3. **Reciprocity**: The principle of reciprocity suggests that people feel obliged to return favors. If customers receive exceptional service or a quality

product, they may feel compelled to reciprocate by leaving a positive review.

4. **Altruism**: Some customers leave reviews out of a genuine desire to help others. They want to share their experiences—good or bad—to guide others in their purchasing decisions.

5. **Personal Benefit**: Reviews can also serve the self-interest of customers. They may leave reviews to earn rewards, gain status within a community, or secure future discounts.

Identifying What Motivates Your Customers

To effectively incentivize reviews, you need to understand what specifically motivates your customer base. Here are some strategies to gain insights:

1. **Surveys and Feedback Forms**: Directly ask your customers what would motivate them to leave a review. Surveys and feedback forms can provide valuable data on customer preferences and expectations.

2. **Customer Personas**: Develop detailed customer personas to understand the demographics, behaviors, and motivations of your audience. Tailor

your incentive programs to align with these personas.

3. **Analyze Past Reviews**: Review the content and context of existing reviews to identify common themes and motivations. Look for patterns in what customers mention and how they express their experiences.

4. **Monitor Social Media**: Social media platforms are rich sources of customer sentiment and behavior. Monitor your brand's mentions and interactions to understand what drives customers to talk about their experiences online.

Aligning Incentives with Customer Values

Once you have a clear understanding of your customers' motivations, you can design incentives that align with their values and expectations. Here are some key considerations:

1. **Relevance**: Ensure that your incentives are relevant and valuable to your customers. For example, offering a discount on a future purchase may be more appealing to loyal customers than a generic reward.

2. **Simplicity**: Keep the process of earning and redeeming incentives simple and straightforward. Complicated procedures can deter customers from participating.

3. **Transparency**: Be transparent about how your incentive program works. Clearly communicate the steps required to earn rewards and any terms and conditions involved.

4. **Personalization**: Personalize your incentives to make them more meaningful. Use customer data to tailor rewards based on past purchases, preferences, and behaviors.

5. **Timeliness**: Timing is crucial. Offer incentives at moments when customers are most likely to leave a review, such as immediately after a positive interaction or a successful purchase.

By understanding the psychological drivers and aligning your incentives with customer values, you can create compelling reasons for your customers to leave positive reviews. In the next chapter, we will explore various types of incentive programs and how to implement them effectively.

Chapter 2: Creating Effective Incentive Programs

Types of Incentives

Offering the right incentives can significantly increase the likelihood of customers leaving positive reviews. There are various types of incentives you can consider, each with its unique benefits and appeal.

1. **Discounts**:
    - **Future Purchase Discounts**: Offering a discount on the customer's next purchase is a straightforward and appealing incentive. It encourages repeat business while rewarding the customer for their review.
    - **Limited-Time Discounts**: Creating a sense of urgency with time-limited discounts can drive faster review submissions.

2. **Freebies and Samples**:
    - **Product Samples**: Providing samples of new or popular products as a reward for reviews can generate excitement and encourage customers to try more of your offerings.
    - **Exclusive Merchandise**: Offering branded merchandise or exclusive items can create a sense of exclusivity and reward loyalty.

3. **Loyalty Points**:
    - **Points for Reviews**: Integrating reviews into your loyalty program by awarding points for each review can incentivize customers who are already engaged in your loyalty scheme.

- **Bonus Points**: Offering additional points for detailed or high-quality reviews can encourage more thoughtful and comprehensive feedback.

4. **Cash Rewards**:
    - **Gift Cards**: Providing gift cards for popular retailers or your own store can be a versatile and attractive incentive.
    - **Cash Back**: Offering a small cash back reward can appeal to customers who prefer direct financial benefits.

5. **Entry into Contests**:
    - **Prize Drawings**: Entering reviewers into a monthly or quarterly drawing for a significant prize can add an element of excitement and competition.
    - **Instant Win Prizes**: Implementing instant win prizes for leaving reviews can create immediate gratification and encourage participation.

Structuring Your Incentive Program

Designing an effective incentive program involves careful planning and execution. Here are key steps to structure your program for maximum impact:

1. **Define Your Goals**:
    - **Specific Objectives**: Clearly outline what you want to achieve with your incentive program, such as increasing the number of

reviews, improving review quality, or boosting overall ratings.
  - **Measurable Metrics**: Determine how you will measure success, whether it's the number of new reviews, customer engagement levels, or increased sales.

2. **Target the Right Audience**:
   - **Segment Your Customers**: Identify which segments of your customer base are most likely to respond to incentives. Tailor your programs to these specific groups to increase effectiveness.
   - **Personalized Offers**: Use customer data to personalize incentives, making them more relevant and attractive to individual customers.

3. **Communicate Clearly**:
   - **Transparent Guidelines**: Clearly explain how customers can participate in the program and what they need to do to earn rewards. Provide step-by-step instructions if necessary.
   - **Consistent Messaging**: Ensure that all your communication channels, including emails, social media, and in-store signage, consistently promote the incentive program.

4. **Monitor and Adjust**:
   - **Track Participation**: Regularly monitor the participation rates and feedback from your

customers. Use this data to assess the program's effectiveness.
- **Make Adjustments**: Be prepared to tweak your incentive program based on customer feedback and performance metrics. This could involve changing the type of incentives, adjusting the value of rewards, or simplifying the process.

Legal Considerations and Ethical Practices

When creating an incentive program, it's essential to consider legal and ethical implications to maintain your brand's integrity and trustworthiness.

1. **Compliance with Laws**:
    - **Review Policies**: Familiarize yourself with the review policies of platforms where your reviews will be posted. Ensure that your incentive program complies with these guidelines.
    - **Disclosure Requirements**: Be transparent about the fact that reviews are incentivized. Many review platforms and consumer protection laws require disclosure of any compensation received for reviews.
2. **Ethical Incentives**:
    - **Authenticity**: Encourage honest reviews by making it clear that both positive and negative feedback are welcome. The goal is to collect genuine opinions that will help other customers.

- **Avoid Manipulation**: Do not attempt to manipulate or filter out negative reviews. This can damage your credibility and lead to repercussions from review platforms.

3. **Fairness**:
    - **Equal Opportunity**: Ensure that all customers have an equal opportunity to participate in the incentive program. Avoid practices that could be perceived as unfair or discriminatory.
    - **Consistent Application**: Apply the same rules and conditions to all participants to maintain fairness and transparency.

By carefully structuring your incentive program and adhering to legal and ethical standards, you can effectively encourage positive reviews while maintaining the trust and loyalty of your customers. In the next chapter, we will explore how to use gamification techniques to further enhance your review incentives.

Chapter 3: Gamification Techniques

Implementing Gamification to Encourage Reviews

Gamification involves applying game-design elements and principles in non-game contexts to motivate and engage users. When it comes to encouraging customer reviews, gamification can make the process more enjoyable and rewarding. Here's how you can incorporate gamification into your review strategy:

1. **Points and Badges**:
    - **Earning Points**: Award points for each review submitted. The more detailed or helpful the review, the more points the customer earns.
    - **Level Up**: Create levels or tiers that customers can achieve by accumulating points. Higher levels could unlock special rewards or privileges.
    - **Badges**: Introduce badges for specific achievements, such as writing a certain number of reviews or receiving 'helpful' votes from other customers.

2. **Leaderboards**:
    - **Competition**: Implement leaderboards that display top reviewers. This can foster a sense of competition and encourage more frequent and detailed reviews.
    - **Recognition**: Recognize top reviewers on your website or social media. Public recognition can be a powerful motivator for customers.

3. **Challenges and Missions**:
    - **Review Challenges**: Create challenges that customers can participate in, such as reviewing multiple products within a month. Successful participants can earn extra points or special rewards.
    - **Missions**: Design missions that involve specific tasks, like taking photos of products or sharing reviews on social media. Completing these missions can provide additional incentives.
4. **Progress Tracking**:
    - **Review Journey**: Allow customers to track their progress in a visually engaging way. A progress bar or journey map can show how close they are to the next reward or level.
    - **Feedback Loops**: Provide instant feedback on reviews submitted, such as points awarded or badges earned. This immediate reinforcement encourages continued participation.

Examples of Successful Gamification Strategies

Looking at real-world examples can provide inspiration for your own gamification efforts. Here are a few successful strategies:

1. **Yelp Elite Squad**:
    - **Exclusive Status**: Yelp's Elite Squad is a prime example of leveraging gamification. Elite members gain special badges,

invitations to exclusive events, and recognition on the platform.

- **Community Engagement**: This program encourages users to write high-quality reviews and engage more actively with the Yelp community.

2. **TripAdvisor Badges and Points**:

    - **Contributor Levels**: TripAdvisor rewards users with points and badges for writing reviews, uploading photos, and getting helpful votes from other users.

    - **Recognition**: Contributors move up through levels (e.g., Novice, Senior Contributor) and can earn recognition and perks, enhancing their status within the community.

3. **Amazon Vine Program**:

    - **Reviewer Ranking**: Amazon ranks its top reviewers and offers them access to the Vine program, where they receive free products in exchange for their reviews.

    - **Incentivized Quality**: This ranking and reward system encourages detailed, high-quality reviews and active participation.

Tools and Platforms to Help Gamify the Review Process

Various tools and platforms can assist you in implementing gamification elements into your review process. Here are some to consider:

1. **Loyalty Programs with Gamification Features**:

- **Yotpo**: This platform offers a comprehensive loyalty program with built-in gamification features like points, rewards, and referral bonuses.
- **Smile.io**: Smile.io allows you to create a loyalty program that includes points, VIP tiers, and referral incentives, all of which can be tailored to include review-related rewards.

2. **Gamification Platforms**:
   - **Bunchball**: Bunchball offers gamification solutions that can be integrated into your existing systems, enabling you to create custom challenges, leaderboards, and rewards for reviews.
   - **Badgeville**: Badgeville provides tools to add gamification elements such as badges, points, and leaderboards to your website or app, enhancing customer engagement and review submissions.

3. **Custom Development**:
   - **In-House Solutions**: If you have development resources, consider building custom gamification features tailored to your specific needs. This allows for greater flexibility and integration with your existing systems.

Best Practices for Gamification in Review Programs

To ensure your gamification efforts are successful, follow these best practices:

1. **Keep it Fun**:
    - **Engaging Design**: Make sure the gamified elements are visually appealing and engaging. The process should be enjoyable and not feel like a chore.
    - **Variety**: Offer a variety of challenges and rewards to keep the program fresh and exciting.

2. **Reward Quality Over Quantity**:
    - **Valuable Reviews**: Encourage detailed, helpful reviews by offering more points or higher rewards for quality content. Avoid incentivizing short or low-effort reviews.
    - **Balanced Incentives**: Ensure that the incentives for quantity do not overshadow the need for high-quality feedback.

3. **Transparency and Fairness**:
    - **Clear Rules**: Clearly communicate the rules and criteria for earning points, badges, and other rewards. Transparency builds trust and encourages participation.
    - **Fair Play**: Monitor the program to prevent abuse or manipulation. Ensure that all participants have a fair chance to earn rewards.

4. **Monitor and Adapt**:

- **Feedback Loop**: Continuously collect feedback from participants to understand what's working and what's not. Use this information to refine and improve your gamification strategies.

- **Data Analysis**: Analyze participation data to identify trends and areas for improvement. Adjust the program as needed to keep it effective and engaging.

By incorporating gamification techniques into your review strategy, you can create a dynamic and engaging experience that motivates customers to share their positive feedback. In the next chapter, we will explore how to leverage social media and your online presence to further drive customer reviews.

Chapter 4: Social Media and Online Presence

Leveraging Social Media to Drive Reviews

Social media platforms are powerful tools for engaging with customers and encouraging reviews. By integrating review requests into your social media strategy, you can reach a wider audience and create more opportunities for customer feedback.

1. **Create Engaging Content**:
    - **Share Customer Stories**: Highlight positive reviews and customer stories on your social media channels. This not only showcases your business's success but also encourages others to share their experiences.
    - **Interactive Posts**: Use polls, questions, and interactive content to engage your audience and prompt them to leave reviews.
2. **Utilize Influencers and Brand Ambassadors**:
    - **Influencer Partnerships**: Collaborate with influencers who can share their experiences with your products or services. Influencers can drive significant traffic to your review pages.
    - **Brand Ambassadors**: Develop a brand ambassador program where loyal customers are rewarded for promoting your brand and leaving reviews.
3. **Run Social Media Campaigns**:
    - **Review Contests**: Organize contests that require participants to leave a review as part

of their entry. Offer attractive prizes to incentivize participation.
- **Hashtag Campaigns**: Create a unique hashtag for your review campaign. Encourage customers to use the hashtag when posting their reviews on social media. This makes it easy to track and share user-generated content.

4. **Encourage User-Generated Content**:
   - **Photo and Video Reviews**: Ask customers to post photos or videos of themselves using your products, accompanied by a review. Visual content is more engaging and can reach a broader audience.
   - **Tagging and Mentions**: Encourage customers to tag your business in their posts. Reposting these mentions on your own social media profiles can amplify their reach and show appreciation.

Running Social Media Contests and Campaigns

Running effective social media contests and campaigns requires careful planning and execution. Here's how to do it:

1. **Define Clear Objectives**:
   - **Goals**: Determine what you want to achieve with your social media contest or campaign. Common goals include increasing the number of reviews, boosting brand

awareness, or engaging with a specific customer segment.
- **Metrics**: Identify the key performance indicators (KPIs) you will use to measure success, such as the number of reviews generated, engagement rates, or social media reach.

2. **Choose the Right Platform**:
   - **Platform Suitability**: Select social media platforms that align with your target audience. For example, Instagram and TikTok are ideal for visual content, while LinkedIn may be more suitable for B2B businesses.
   - **Cross-Platform Promotion**: Promote your contest or campaign across multiple platforms to maximize reach. Use consistent messaging and branding to create a cohesive campaign.

3. **Create Compelling Content**:
   - **Visual Appeal**: Design eye-catching graphics and videos to promote your contest or campaign. High-quality visuals are more likely to capture attention and encourage participation.
   - **Clear Instructions**: Provide clear and concise instructions on how to participate. Include details on how to submit reviews, use hashtags, or tag your business.

4. **Offer Attractive Prizes**:
    - **Valuable Rewards**: Choose prizes that are valuable and relevant to your audience. Popular options include gift cards, exclusive products, or experiences.
    - **Tiered Prizes**: Consider offering tiered prizes to reward different levels of participation. This can motivate more customers to join in and increase overall engagement.

5. **Promote Widely**:
    - **Organic Promotion**: Share your contest or campaign through organic posts, stories, and live sessions. Engage with your audience by responding to comments and questions.
    - **Paid Advertising**: Use paid social media advertising to boost the visibility of your contest or campaign. Target specific demographics to reach potential participants.

Encouraging Reviews Through Influencer Partnerships

Influencer partnerships can be a highly effective way to drive customer reviews. Influencers have established trust with their followers, making their recommendations powerful. Here's how to leverage influencer partnerships:

1. **Identify the Right Influencers**:
    - **Relevance**: Choose influencers whose audience aligns with your target market. Their followers should have an interest in your products or services.

- **Authenticity**: Look for influencers who have a genuine connection with their audience. Authentic endorsements are more likely to result in credible reviews.

2. **Establish Clear Agreements**:

    - **Expectations**: Clearly outline the expectations for the partnership, including the type of content to be created, the platforms to be used, and the timeline for posts.

    - **Compensation**: Agree on fair compensation for the influencer's efforts. This could be monetary payment, free products, or other incentives.

3. **Provide Creative Freedom**:

    - **Authentic Content**: Allow influencers to create content in their own style. Authentic, relatable content resonates more with their followers and increases the likelihood of positive reviews.

    - **Guidelines**: Provide guidelines to ensure the content aligns with your brand's values and messaging, but avoid being overly prescriptive.

4. **Track and Measure Results**:

    - **Performance Metrics**: Use tracking links, unique hashtags, and social media analytics to measure the performance of the influencer campaign.

- **Review Generation**: Monitor the number and quality of reviews generated as a result of the partnership. Adjust future campaigns based on these insights.

Utilizing Social Media Reviews

Once you've gathered reviews through social media, it's important to leverage them effectively:

1. **Showcase Reviews on Your Website**:
   - **Testimonials**: Highlight positive reviews and testimonials on your website. This adds credibility and can influence potential customers' purchasing decisions.
   - **Review Widgets**: Use review widgets or plugins to display real-time social media reviews on your website. This keeps the content fresh and dynamic.

2. **Share Reviews Across Platforms**:
   - **Content Sharing**: Share positive reviews and user-generated content across your social media channels. This not only recognizes the customer but also provides social proof to other potential buyers.
   - **Highlight Stories**: Create highlight reels or story highlights on platforms like Instagram to showcase customer reviews. This makes it easy for new visitors to see what others are saying about your brand.

3. **Engage with Reviewers**:

- **Respond to Reviews**: Engage with customers who leave reviews by thanking them and responding to their feedback. This shows that you value their input and encourages others to leave reviews as well.
- **Feature Reviewers**: Occasionally feature reviewers in your posts or stories. This can incentivize more customers to leave reviews in the hope of being featured.

By leveraging social media and your online presence, you can create a dynamic and interactive platform for collecting and showcasing customer reviews. In the next chapter, we will explore how to offer exclusive offers and discounts as incentives for leaving reviews.

Chapter 5: Exclusive Offers and Discounts

Offering Special Discounts for Reviews

Discounts are a popular and effective way to incentivize customers to leave reviews. When done correctly, they not only encourage feedback but also promote repeat business.

1. **Future Purchase Discounts**:
    - **Standard Discounts**: Offer a percentage or fixed amount off the next purchase. For example, "Leave a review and get 10% off your next order."
    - **Conditional Discounts**: Tie discounts to specific conditions, such as a minimum purchase amount. This encourages customers to spend more.

2. **Limited-Time Offers**:
    - **Urgency**: Create a sense of urgency by offering discounts that are valid for a limited time. For instance, "Leave a review within the next 7 days and receive a 15% discount."
    - **Seasonal Discounts**: Align your discount offers with seasonal events or holidays to make them more appealing.

3. **Exclusive Member Discounts**:
    - **Loyalty Program Integration**: Integrate review incentives into your existing loyalty program. Offer exclusive discounts to members who leave reviews.
    - **Tiered Rewards**: Provide tiered discounts based on the number or quality of reviews.

For example, "Get 5% off for your first review, 10% off for your third review."

Creating Exclusive Deals for Repeat Reviewers

To foster ongoing engagement and loyalty, consider offering exclusive deals for customers who consistently leave reviews.

1. **Cumulative Discounts**:
   - **Accumulative Offers**: Increase the discount value with each additional review. For example, "Leave your first review and get 5% off, your second review and get 10% off, and so on."
   - **Milestone Rewards**: Celebrate review milestones with special discounts. For instance, "Leave 5 reviews and get 20% off your next purchase."
2. **Special Access to Sales**:
   - **Early Access**: Grant early access to sales or new product launches to customers who leave reviews. This makes them feel valued and encourages them to stay engaged.
   - **Exclusive Sales**: Host exclusive sales events for top reviewers, offering significant discounts as a reward for their contributions.
3. **Bundled Offers**:
   - **Product Bundles**: Offer discounted bundles or packages as a reward for reviews. For

example, "Leave a review and get 20% off any bundle."

- o **Add-On Discounts**: Provide discounts on add-on products or accessories when a customer leaves a review of the main product.

Timing Your Offers for the Best Response Rates

The timing of your discount offers can greatly influence their effectiveness. Consider the following strategies to maximize response rates:

1. **Post-Purchase Timing**:

    - o **Immediate Follow-Up**: Send an email or notification shortly after purchase, requesting a review and offering a discount as a thank-you. This capitalizes on the customer's recent positive experience.
    - o **Usage-Based Timing**: Allow some time for the customer to use the product before requesting a review. This can lead to more detailed and authentic feedback.

2. **Event-Based Timing**:

    - o **Anniversaries**: Mark the anniversary of the customer's first purchase or review with a special discount offer.
    - o **Product Updates**: When you release a new version or update of a product, offer discounts to customers who review the previous version.

3. **Behavioral Triggers**:
    - **Engagement-Based Offers**: Use customer behavior data to trigger discount offers. For example, if a customer frequently visits your review page but hasn't left a review, send them a personalized discount offer.
    - **Abandoned Cart Recovery**: If a customer abandons their cart, send a follow-up email that includes a discount offer in exchange for a review of a previous purchase.

Best Practices for Offering Discounts as Incentives

To ensure your discount offers are effective and well-received, follow these best practices:

1. **Clear Communication**:
    - **Transparent Terms**: Clearly explain the terms and conditions of the discount offer, including any minimum purchase requirements or expiration dates.
    - **Simple Redemption**: Make it easy for customers to redeem their discounts. Provide clear instructions and avoid complicated procedures.

2. **Personalization**:
    - **Tailored Offers**: Personalize discount offers based on the customer's purchase history and preferences. This increases the perceived value of the offer.

- **Dynamic Discounts**: Use dynamic pricing to offer different discount levels based on customer segments or behavior.

3. **Tracking and Analysis**:
    - **Monitor Performance**: Track the performance of your discount offers to see which ones are most effective in generating reviews.
    - **Adjust Strategies**: Use the data collected to refine and adjust your discount strategies over time. Continuously test different offers to find the most successful approaches.

4. **Maintain Quality and Authenticity**:
    - **Encourage Honest Reviews**: Make it clear that customers should leave honest reviews, regardless of whether they are positive or negative. Authentic feedback is more valuable and trustworthy.
    - **Avoid Over-Incentivizing**: Be cautious not to offer discounts that are too large, as this might incentivize low-effort reviews. Balance the value of the discount with the effort required to leave a meaningful review.

By offering exclusive discounts and timing your offers strategically, you can effectively encourage more customers to leave positive reviews. In the next chapter, we will explore how to integrate reviews into your loyalty programs and reward systems.

Chapter 6: Loyalty Programs and Rewards

Integrating Reviews into Your Loyalty Program

Loyalty programs are powerful tools for building long-term relationships with customers. By integrating review incentives into your loyalty program, you can encourage more reviews while rewarding customer loyalty.

1. **Points for Reviews**:
    - **Earning Points**: Award loyalty points for each review submitted. For example, "Earn 50 points for every review you leave."
    - **Quality Reviews**: Offer additional points for detailed and helpful reviews. This encourages customers to put more effort into their feedback.
2. **Review Milestones**:
    - **Milestone Rewards**: Recognize customers who reach review milestones with special rewards. For instance, "Leave 10 reviews and receive a free product."
    - **Tiered Levels**: Create tiered levels within your loyalty program that customers can achieve by leaving reviews. Higher tiers unlock exclusive benefits and rewards.
3. **Bonus Points for Featured Reviews**:
    - **Featured Reviews**: Select and highlight the best reviews each month. Award bonus points to customers whose reviews are featured on your website or social media.
    - **Engagement Rewards**: Encourage customers to engage with each other's reviews by offering points for upvotes or helpful ratings.

Offering Tiered Rewards Based on Review Frequency

Tiered rewards provide an additional layer of motivation for customers to leave reviews regularly. Here's how to implement tiered rewards effectively:

1. **Basic Tier**:
    - **Initial Reward**: Offer a small reward for the first review, such as a few loyalty points or a minor discount. This encourages customers to take the first step.
    - **Accessible Milestones**: Set easily achievable milestones to maintain momentum and engagement.
2. **Intermediate Tier**:
    - **Enhanced Rewards**: Increase the value of rewards as customers progress to higher tiers. For example, offer larger discounts, more points, or exclusive access to sales.
    - **Recognition**: Provide special recognition to intermediate-tier customers, such as a badge or shoutout on social media.
3. **Advanced Tier**:
    - **Premium Rewards**: Reserve the most valuable rewards for advanced-tier customers. These could include significant discounts, free products, or exclusive experiences.
    - **Exclusive Benefits**: Offer exclusive benefits such as early access to new products, invitations to special events, or personalized customer service.

Examples of Effective Loyalty Programs

Looking at successful loyalty programs can provide inspiration for your own efforts. Here are a few examples:

1. **Sephora Beauty Insider**:
   - **Points System**: Sephora's Beauty Insider program allows customers to earn points for every purchase and review. Points can be redeemed for beauty products, experiences, and more.
   - **Tiered Rewards**: The program has tiered levels (Insider, VIB, Rouge) that offer increasing benefits and exclusive rewards as customers spend more and engage with the brand.
2. **Starbucks Rewards**:
   - **Stars for Reviews**: Starbucks Rewards members earn stars for purchases and reviews, which can be redeemed for free drinks and food.
   - **Bonus Star Opportunities**: The program frequently offers bonus star opportunities for specific actions, such as writing a review or participating in a promotion.
3. **Amazon Prime**:
   - **Review Incentives**: Amazon Prime members often receive incentives for leaving reviews, such as early access to deals or additional points in the Amazon Rewards program.
   - **Exclusive Access**: Prime members enjoy exclusive access to products and services, creating a sense of privilege and loyalty.

Best Practices for Integrating Reviews into Loyalty Programs

To ensure your loyalty program effectively incentivizes reviews, follow these best practices:

1. **Seamless Integration**:
   - **User-Friendly**: Make it easy for customers to leave reviews and track their points within your loyalty program. Simplify the process with a user-friendly interface.
   - **Consistent Experience**: Ensure that the review process is consistent across all touchpoints, whether online or in-store.
2. **Clear Communication**:
   - **Transparent Terms**: Clearly communicate the rules and benefits of earning points through reviews. Transparency builds trust and encourages participation.
   - **Regular Updates**: Keep customers informed about their progress and upcoming rewards. Regular updates maintain engagement and excitement.
3. **Personalization**:
   - **Tailored Rewards**: Personalize rewards based on customer preferences and behavior. Use data analytics to understand what motivates your customers and offer relevant incentives.
   - **Dynamic Offers**: Implement dynamic offers that adjust based on customer interactions and engagement levels.
4. **Monitor and Adapt**:
   - **Feedback Loop**: Continuously collect feedback from customers about their experience with the loyalty program. Use this feedback to make improvements and adjustments.
   - **Performance Analysis**: Analyze the performance of your loyalty program to identify trends and areas for improvement.

Adjust your strategies based on data insights.

By integrating reviews into your loyalty program and offering tiered rewards, you can create a compelling incentive for customers to leave positive feedback. In the next chapter, we will explore personalized experiences and how they can enhance your review incentive strategy.

Chapter 7: Personalized Experiences

Personalizing Incentives to Match Customer Preferences

Personalized experiences can significantly enhance the effectiveness of your review incentives by making customers feel valued and understood. By tailoring your incentives to individual preferences, you can foster stronger connections and encourage more meaningful feedback.

1. **Leverage Customer Data**:
    - **Purchase History**: Use data on customers' past purchases to offer relevant incentives. For example, if a customer frequently buys skincare products, offer a free sample of a new skincare item for their review.
    - **Browsing Behavior**: Analyze browsing behavior to understand customer interests. Send personalized review requests for products they have shown interest in but haven't purchased yet.
2. **Segment Your Audience**:
    - **Demographic Segmentation**: Tailor incentives based on demographic factors such as age, gender, and location. For instance, younger customers might prefer social media shoutouts, while older customers may appreciate exclusive discounts.
    - **Behavioral Segmentation**: Group customers based on their behavior, such as frequency of purchases, loyalty program status, or review activity. Offer incentives that match their engagement level.
3. **Customized Messaging**:
    - **Personalized Emails**: Craft personalized email requests that address customers by

name and reference their specific interactions with your brand. This shows that you value their individual contributions.
- **Targeted Offers**: Include personalized offers in your review requests. For example, "Hi [Name], we hope you're enjoying your recent purchase of [Product]. Leave a review and receive a 20% discount on your next order of [Related Product]."

Using Data and Feedback to Tailor Your Approach

To effectively personalize your review incentives, it's crucial to gather and utilize customer data and feedback. Here's how to do it:

1. **Collect Comprehensive Data**:
   - **Customer Profiles**: Build detailed customer profiles that include purchase history, preferences, and engagement data. Use CRM systems to manage and analyze this information.
   - **Feedback Forms**: Include questions about customer preferences and interests in your feedback forms. This data can help you create more relevant incentives.
2. **Analyze Feedback**:
   - **Sentiment Analysis**: Use sentiment analysis tools to gauge the tone and sentiment of customer reviews. This can help you understand customer satisfaction levels and tailor incentives accordingly.
   - **Behavioral Insights**: Analyze patterns in customer behavior, such as which incentives lead to the most reviews and what types of

reviews are submitted. Use these insights to refine your approach.
3. **Test and Iterate**:
    o **A/B Testing**: Conduct A/B tests to compare different types of personalized incentives and messaging. Determine which strategies are most effective and adjust your campaigns accordingly.
    o **Continuous Improvement**: Continuously monitor the performance of your personalized incentives and make data-driven adjustments. Stay agile and responsive to customer feedback and preferences.

Building Long-Term Relationships Through Personalized Incentives

Personalized incentives can play a significant role in building long-term customer relationships. By consistently showing that you understand and value your customers, you can foster loyalty and encourage ongoing engagement.

1. **Consistent Engagement**:
    o **Regular Communication**: Maintain regular communication with your customers through personalized emails, messages, and social media interactions. Keep them informed about new products, special offers, and review opportunities.
    o **Loyalty Rewards**: Integrate personalized review incentives into your loyalty program, offering ongoing rewards for consistent engagement and feedback.
2. **Exclusive Experiences**:

- **VIP Programs**: Create VIP programs that offer exclusive experiences and rewards for top reviewers. This could include early access to new products, special events, or personalized customer service.
- **Customized Offers**: Regularly offer customized discounts and promotions based on individual customer preferences and past behavior. Show customers that you recognize their unique tastes and needs.

3. **Meaningful Interactions**:
   - **Personal Touch**: Add a personal touch to your interactions with customers. Handwritten thank-you notes, personalized follow-ups, and thoughtful gestures can leave a lasting impression.
   - **Feedback Acknowledgment**: Publicly acknowledge and thank customers for their reviews. Highlighting their contributions on your website or social media can make them feel appreciated and valued.

Examples of Successful Personalized Incentive Programs

Here are a few examples of brands that have successfully implemented personalized incentive programs:

1. **Amazon**:
   - **Personalized Recommendations**: Amazon uses customer purchase and browsing data to offer personalized product recommendations and incentives. Customers receive tailored review requests based on their purchase history.

- **Targeted Discounts**: Amazon often provides personalized discounts on items customers have shown interest in, encouraging them to leave reviews for these products.

2. **Netflix**:
    - **Customized Content**: Netflix uses viewing history to personalize content recommendations and incentivize reviews. Subscribers receive requests to rate and review shows and movies they've watched, enhancing their viewing experience.
    - **Tailored Messaging**: Personalized emails and in-app notifications prompt users to leave reviews for content they've enjoyed, making the review process more relevant and engaging.

3. **Starbucks**:
    - **Personalized Offers**: Starbucks Rewards members receive personalized offers based on their purchase history and preferences. This includes special discounts, free drinks, and early access to new products.
    - **Engagement-Based Rewards**: Starbucks incentivizes reviews by offering bonus stars and exclusive rewards for members who provide feedback on their experiences.

By leveraging personalized experiences and incentives, you can create a more engaging and rewarding review process for your customers. In the next chapter, we will explore how to organize contests and giveaways to further incentivize reviews and drive customer engagement.

Chapter 8: Contests and Giveaways

Organizing Review-Based Contests

Contests are an exciting way to encourage customer reviews while engaging your audience. When designed effectively, they can boost participation, generate buzz, and increase the number of positive reviews.

1. **Define Clear Objectives**:
    - **Specific Goals**: Set clear objectives for your contest, such as increasing the number of reviews, improving review quality, or boosting brand awareness.
    - **Measurable Metrics**: Determine how you will measure success, whether it's through the number of new reviews, engagement rates, or increased social media activity.
2. **Choose Attractive Prizes**:
    - **Relevant Rewards**: Select prizes that resonate with your target audience. Popular options include gift cards, free products, exclusive experiences, or significant discounts.
    - **Tiered Prizes**: Offer multiple prize levels to encourage participation. For example, have a grand prize for the best review and smaller prizes for runner-ups or random participants.
3. **Set Clear Rules and Guidelines**:
    - **Eligibility**: Clearly define who is eligible to participate in the contest. This could include existing customers, new customers, or members of your loyalty program.
    - **Submission Guidelines**: Provide clear instructions on how to submit reviews, including where to post them and what criteria they should meet (e.g., length, detail, including photos).

4. **Promote Widely**:
   - **Multi-Channel Promotion**: Promote your contest across all your communication channels, including email, social media, your website, and in-store signage.
   - **Consistent Messaging**: Ensure your contest messaging is consistent and highlights the key benefits and how to participate.
5. **Engage Participants**:
   - **Regular Updates**: Keep participants engaged by providing regular updates on the contest, such as how many entries have been received and reminders about the deadline.
   - **Acknowledge Entries**: Publicly acknowledge and thank participants for their reviews. This can be done through social media shoutouts or email updates.

Rules and Regulations for Fair Contests

Ensuring your contest is fair and compliant with legal requirements is crucial to maintaining trust and credibility.

1. **Legal Compliance**:
   - **Review Platform Policies**: Familiarize yourself with the policies of review platforms where your contest will be promoted to ensure compliance.
   - **State and Federal Laws**: Ensure your contest complies with all relevant state and federal laws, including rules about sweepstakes, contests, and lotteries.
2. **Transparency**:
   - **Clear Terms and Conditions**: Provide detailed terms and conditions that outline how the contest works, including entry

methods, eligibility, judging criteria, and prize distribution.
    - **Disclosure**: Clearly disclose that reviews submitted as part of the contest are incentivized. This maintains transparency and trust with both participants and potential customers.
3. **Judging Criteria**:
    - **Objective Criteria**: Establish clear and objective criteria for judging entries. This could include the quality and detail of the review, creativity, and the inclusion of photos or videos.
    - **Independent Judging**: Consider using an independent panel of judges or a random drawing to select winners to ensure fairness and avoid any perception of bias.

Promoting Your Contests for Maximum Participation

Effective promotion is key to maximizing participation in your contests. Here are some strategies to boost visibility and engagement:

1. **Social Media Campaigns**:
    - **Hashtags**: Create a unique contest hashtag to track entries and generate buzz. Encourage participants to use the hashtag in their submissions.
    - **Influencer Partnerships**: Partner with influencers to promote your contest to their followers. Influencers can help reach a broader audience and lend credibility to your campaign.
2. **Email Marketing**:

- **Targeted Emails**: Send personalized email invitations to your customer base, highlighting the benefits of participating and the prizes on offer.
- **Follow-Up Reminders**: Send follow-up emails as the contest deadline approaches to remind customers to participate and keep the excitement alive.

3. **Website and Blog**:
   - **Dedicated Landing Page**: Create a dedicated landing page on your website with all the details about the contest, including how to enter, rules, and prizes.
   - **Blog Posts**: Write blog posts about the contest, including tips for writing great reviews, previous contest winners, and updates on the current contest.

4. **In-Store Promotion**:
   - **Signage**: Use in-store signage to promote the contest to customers who visit your physical locations.
   - **Staff Engagement**: Train your staff to inform customers about the contest and encourage them to participate.

Examples of Successful Contests

Here are a few examples of successful review-based contests to inspire your own efforts:

1. **TripAdvisor's Review Contest**:
   - **Seasonal Themes**: TripAdvisor runs seasonal review contests, encouraging users to share their travel experiences during peak travel times. Prizes include travel vouchers and exclusive experiences.

- **Engaging Content**: The contests often require participants to include photos or videos, making the reviews more engaging and valuable to other users.
2. **Yelp's Review Challenge**:
    - **Local Focus**: Yelp often organizes local review challenges, encouraging users to review businesses in their area. Prizes include gift cards to local businesses and exclusive Yelp merchandise.
    - **Community Building**: These challenges help build a sense of community among Yelp users and support local businesses.
3. **Amazon's Vine Program**:
    - **Product Testing**: Amazon's Vine program selects top reviewers to receive free products in exchange for honest reviews. This incentivizes high-quality feedback and helps new products gain visibility.
    - **Recognition and Rewards**: Vine members are recognized as trusted reviewers, which adds credibility to their reviews and enhances their reputation within the Amazon community.

Best Practices for Running Successful Contests

To ensure your contests are successful and well-received, follow these best practices:

1. **Plan Thoroughly**:
    - **Detailed Planning**: Plan every aspect of your contest in detail, from objectives and prizes to promotion and judging. A well-thought-out plan ensures a smooth execution.

- **Contingency Plans**: Be prepared for potential issues, such as low participation or technical difficulties. Have contingency plans in place to address these challenges.

2. **Engage Continuously**:
    - **Ongoing Engagement**: Keep participants engaged throughout the contest period with regular updates, reminders, and interactions. This maintains excitement and encourages continued participation.
    - **Post-Contest Follow-Up**: After the contest ends, follow up with participants to thank them for their involvement and share the results. This helps maintain a positive relationship with your audience.
3. **Measure and Learn**:
    - **Analyze Results**: Measure the success of your contest by analyzing key metrics, such as the number of entries, engagement rates, and the quality of reviews.
    - **Feedback and Improvement**: Gather feedback from participants and use it to improve future contests. Continuously refine your strategies based on what works best.

By organizing engaging contests and giveaways, you can create excitement around your brand, encourage more customer reviews, and build a loyal community. In the next chapter, we will explore collaborative incentives and how to partner with other businesses for joint incentives.

Chapter 9: Collaborative Incentives

Partnering with Other Businesses for Joint Incentives

Collaborative incentives involve partnering with other businesses to offer joint rewards for customer reviews. These partnerships can help you reach new audiences, enhance the value of your incentives, and build strong business relationships.

1. **Identify Compatible Partners**:
    - **Complementary Products**: Look for businesses that offer complementary products or services. For example, a restaurant might partner with a local bakery, or a fitness center with a health food store.
    - **Shared Audience**: Choose partners that share a similar target audience. This ensures that the incentives are relevant and attractive to both customer bases.
2. **Develop Joint Incentives**:
    - **Bundled Offers**: Create bundled offers that include products or services from both businesses. For instance, a spa and a beauty salon might offer a combined discount on massages and facials.
    - **Cross-Promotions**: Promote each other's products or services through joint discounts or special offers. A bookstore and a coffee shop could offer a discount on coffee with the purchase of a book and vice versa.
3. **Coordinate Marketing Efforts**:

- **Joint Campaigns**: Run joint marketing campaigns to promote the collaborative incentives. Use combined branding in social media posts, email newsletters, and website banners.
- **Shared Content**: Create shared content, such as blog posts, videos, or social media takeovers, to highlight the partnership and the benefits of the joint incentives.

Cross-Promotions to Reach a Wider Audience

Cross-promotions involve promoting your partner's products or services alongside your own, helping both businesses reach a wider audience and drive more reviews.

1. **Social Media Collaborations**:
    - **Guest Posts**: Exchange guest posts on each other's social media accounts. This can introduce your brand to your partner's followers and vice versa.
    - **Joint Contests**: Run joint social media contests where participants must engage with both brands. This can significantly increase visibility and engagement for both businesses.
2. **Email Marketing**:
    - **Co-Branded Newsletters**: Feature your partner's products or services in your email newsletters, and ask them to do the same. Highlight the benefits of the collaborative

incentive and encourage customers to leave reviews.
- **Referral Programs**: Create referral programs where customers are rewarded for referring your partner's business and vice versa. This can drive new customers and increase review submissions.

3. **In-Store Promotions**:
    - **Shared Signage**: Display promotional materials for your partner's business in your store, and ask them to do the same. Include information about the joint incentives and how to participate.
    - **Collaborative Events**: Host joint events, such as workshops, pop-up shops, or customer appreciation days. These events can attract a broader audience and provide opportunities for gathering reviews.

Case Studies of Successful Collaborations

Examining successful collaborations can provide inspiration and insights for your own joint incentive programs. Here are a few examples:

1. **Starbucks and Spotify**:
    - **Enhanced Customer Experience**: Starbucks partnered with Spotify to offer a unique music experience in its stores. Starbucks customers who left reviews on Spotify playlists received discounts on their next coffee purchase.

- **Cross-Promotional Success**: This partnership allowed both brands to enhance their customer experience and reach a wider audience through cross-promotion.

2. **Uber and Spotify**:
   - **Personalized Ride Experience**: Uber and Spotify collaborated to allow riders to control the music during their Uber rides. Riders who left reviews about their music experience received credits for future rides.
   - **Increased Engagement**: This partnership increased user engagement for both Uber and Spotify and provided a memorable and personalized experience for customers.

3. **Nike and Apple**:
   - **Integrated Products**: Nike and Apple collaborated to integrate the Nike+ app with Apple devices. Customers who reviewed the app and shared their fitness achievements received discounts on Nike products.
   - **Shared Audience**: This partnership leveraged the shared audience of fitness enthusiasts and tech-savvy consumers, driving engagement and reviews for both brands.

Best Practices for Collaborative Incentives

To ensure your collaborative incentive programs are successful, follow these best practices:

1. **Clear Communication**:

- **Aligned Goals**: Ensure that both businesses have aligned goals and a clear understanding of the objectives of the partnership.
- **Transparent Agreements**: Establish clear agreements regarding the roles, responsibilities, and benefits for each partner. Document these agreements to avoid misunderstandings.

2. **Consistent Branding**:
    - **Unified Messaging**: Maintain consistent branding and messaging across all promotional materials. This ensures a cohesive experience for customers and reinforces the partnership.
    - **Mutual Promotion**: Both businesses should actively promote the joint incentives. Mutual promotion increases visibility and reinforces the collaborative nature of the program.

3. **Monitor and Evaluate**:
    - **Performance Metrics**: Track the performance of the collaborative incentives, including the number of reviews generated, customer engagement levels, and sales impact.
    - **Feedback and Improvement**: Collect feedback from customers and partners to understand what worked well and what can be improved. Use this feedback to refine future collaborations.

By partnering with other businesses for joint incentives, you can expand your reach, enhance the value of your offers, and drive more customer reviews. In the next chapter, we will explore the role of technology and automation in managing your review incentives effectively.

Chapter 10: Technology and Automation

Utilizing CRM and Automation Tools to Manage Incentives

Customer Relationship Management (CRM) and automation tools can streamline the process of managing review incentives, ensuring that your efforts are efficient, consistent, and scalable.

1. **CRM Integration**:
    - **Centralized Data**: Use a CRM system to centralize customer data, including purchase history, review activity, and preferences. This allows you to track and manage your incentive programs more effectively.
    - **Segmentation**: Segment your customer base within the CRM based on relevant criteria such as purchase behavior, engagement level, and past review activity. This enables you to target your incentives more precisely.
2. **Automation Tools**:
    - **Automated Emails**: Set up automated email campaigns to request reviews after a purchase. Customize the timing and content based on customer data to make the requests more personalized and relevant.
    - **Triggered Responses**: Use automation to trigger responses based on customer actions. For example, send a thank-you email with a discount code immediately after a review is submitted.
3. **Loyalty Program Integration**:
    - **Points Tracking**: Integrate your loyalty program with your CRM to automatically track points earned from reviews. This ensures accuracy and reduces manual effort.

- **Reward Redemption**: Automate the process of reward redemption by linking it to your CRM. When customers earn enough points, automatically notify them and provide instructions for redeeming their rewards.

Tracking and Analyzing the Effectiveness of Your Programs

To continuously improve your review incentive programs, it's crucial to track their performance and analyze the results. Here are key metrics and methods to consider:

1. **Key Performance Indicators (KPIs)**:
   - **Number of Reviews**: Track the total number of reviews submitted as a result of your incentive programs. This is a direct measure of their impact.
   - **Review Quality**: Monitor the quality of reviews by assessing their detail, helpfulness, and rating scores. High-quality reviews are more valuable than simple, short reviews.
   - **Customer Engagement**: Measure engagement levels, such as email open rates, click-through rates, and social media interactions related to your review requests.
2. **Analytics Tools**:
   - **Google Analytics**: Use Google Analytics to track traffic to your review pages and the conversion rates from your incentive campaigns. This helps you understand which channels and messages are most effective.
   - **Social Media Analytics**: Monitor social media metrics to gauge the reach and impact

of your review-related posts and campaigns. Track metrics like likes, shares, comments, and hashtag usage.
3. **Customer Feedback**:
    o **Surveys and Polls**: Use surveys and polls to gather feedback from customers about their experience with your incentive programs. This can provide insights into what motivates them and how you can improve.
    o **Direct Feedback**: Encourage customers to provide direct feedback on your review process and incentives. This can reveal pain points and areas for enhancement.

Best Practices for Integrating Technology into Your Strategy

To maximize the benefits of technology and automation in your review incentive strategy, follow these best practices:

1. **Data Accuracy**:
    o **Clean Data**: Regularly clean and update your customer data to ensure accuracy. Remove duplicates and correct any inaccuracies to maintain the integrity of your CRM.
    o **Data Privacy**: Ensure that you comply with data privacy regulations, such as GDPR or CCPA. Protect customer data and be transparent about how it is used.
2. **Personalization**:
    o **Customized Communication**: Use customer data to personalize your communication. Address customers by name and reference their specific interactions with your brand.

- **Relevant Incentives**: Tailor your incentives to match customer preferences and behaviors. Personalized incentives are more likely to resonate and drive action.
3. **Continuous Improvement**:
    - **A/B Testing**: Conduct A/B tests to compare different incentive strategies and messages. Use the results to refine your approach and improve effectiveness.
    - **Regular Reviews**: Regularly review the performance of your incentive programs and make data-driven adjustments. Stay agile and responsive to changing customer needs and market trends.

Tools and Platforms to Enhance Your Incentive Programs

Various tools and platforms can help you manage and enhance your review incentive programs. Here are some recommended options:

1. **Email Marketing Tools**:
    - **Mailchimp**: Mailchimp offers robust email marketing automation features, including triggered emails and personalized campaigns. It integrates well with most CRM systems.
    - **Klaviyo**: Klaviyo is another powerful email marketing tool that allows for highly personalized and data-driven email campaigns. It's particularly strong in e-commerce integrations.
2. **CRM Systems**:
    - **Salesforce**: Salesforce is a leading CRM platform with extensive features for

customer data management, segmentation, and automation. It's highly customizable and scalable.
- **HubSpot**: HubSpot offers a comprehensive CRM solution with integrated marketing, sales, and service tools. Its user-friendly interface and automation capabilities make it a popular choice for businesses of all sizes.

3. **Review Management Platforms**:
    - **Trustpilot**: Trustpilot is a review management platform that helps businesses collect, manage, and display customer reviews. It offers integrations with CRM systems and automation tools.
    - **Yotpo**: Yotpo provides a suite of tools for review collection, loyalty programs, and user-generated content. It integrates with major e-commerce platforms and CRM systems.

By leveraging technology and automation, you can streamline the management of your review incentive programs, track their effectiveness, and continuously improve your strategies. In the final chapter, we will recap the key points and provide actionable steps for implementing your review incentive programs.

Conclusion: Implementing Your Review Incentive Programs

Recap of Key Points

Throughout this eBook, we've explored various strategies and best practices for incentivizing customer reviews. Here's a recap of the key points covered:

1. **Understanding Customer Motivation**:
    - Recognize the psychological factors driving customers to leave reviews, such as the need for recognition, social proof, reciprocity, altruism, and personal benefit.
    - Identify what specifically motivates your customer base to tailor your incentive programs effectively.

2. **Creating Effective Incentive Programs**:
    - Offer a variety of incentives, including discounts, freebies, loyalty points, cash rewards, and entry into contests.
    - Structure your programs with clear goals, target the right audience, and communicate transparently.

3. **Gamification Techniques**:
    - Implement gamification elements like points, badges, leaderboards, challenges, and missions to make the review process engaging and fun.
    - Use real-world examples and tools to successfully gamify your review incentives.

4. **Social Media and Online Presence**:

- Leverage social media to drive reviews by creating engaging content, collaborating with influencers, running campaigns, and encouraging user-generated content.
- Promote your review incentives through various channels for maximum participation.

5. **Exclusive Offers and Discounts**:
    - Offer special discounts and exclusive deals for customers who leave reviews.
    - Time your offers strategically to maximize response rates and maintain customer engagement.

6. **Loyalty Programs and Rewards**:
    - Integrate review incentives into your loyalty programs with tiered rewards and milestone recognition.
    - Use successful examples to design and implement effective loyalty-based review incentives.

7. **Personalized Experiences**:
    - Personalize incentives to match customer preferences using data and feedback.
    - Build long-term relationships through consistent engagement, exclusive experiences, and meaningful interactions.

8. **Contests and Giveaways**:

- Organize review-based contests with attractive prizes and clear rules.
- Promote your contests widely and ensure they are fair and compliant with regulations.

9. **Collaborative Incentives**:
    - Partner with other businesses for joint incentives to reach new audiences and enhance value.
    - Use cross-promotions and shared marketing efforts to maximize the impact of collaborative incentives.

10. **Technology and Automation**:
    - Utilize CRM and automation tools to manage and streamline your incentive programs.
    - Track and analyze the effectiveness of your programs using key metrics and continuous improvement practices.

Actionable Steps for Implementing Your Programs

Now that you have a comprehensive understanding of review incentives, it's time to put these strategies into action. Follow these steps to implement your review incentive programs effectively:

1. **Set Clear Objectives**:
    - Define what you want to achieve with your review incentive programs, such as increasing the number of reviews, improving review quality, or boosting customer loyalty.

2. **Choose the Right Incentives:**
    - Select incentives that resonate with your target audience. Consider a mix of discounts, freebies, loyalty points, contests, and personalized offers.

3. **Develop a Detailed Plan:**
    - Create a detailed plan that outlines the structure of your incentive programs, including eligibility criteria, reward types, communication strategies, and timelines.

4. **Integrate Technology:**
    - Use CRM and automation tools to manage customer data, track participation, and streamline your incentive processes. Ensure seamless integration with your existing systems.

5. **Promote Widely:**
    - Promote your incentive programs through multiple channels, including email marketing, social media, your website, and in-store signage. Use consistent messaging to reinforce your campaign.

6. **Monitor and Adjust:**
    - Regularly monitor the performance of your incentive programs using key metrics. Gather feedback from customers and make data-driven adjustments to improve effectiveness.

7. **Engage Continuously**:
    - Maintain ongoing engagement with your customers by providing regular updates, acknowledging their contributions, and offering new incentives to keep them motivated.

8. **Evaluate and Refine**:
    - Periodically evaluate the overall impact of your review incentive programs. Use insights from your analysis to refine your strategies and ensure continuous improvement.

Final Thoughts

Incentivizing customer reviews is a powerful way to boost your brand's credibility, attract new customers, and foster loyalty. By understanding what motivates your customers and implementing well-designed incentive programs, you can encourage more positive reviews and create a thriving community of satisfied customers.

Remember, the key to success lies in offering relevant and meaningful incentives, maintaining transparency, and continuously engaging with your audience. With the strategies and best practices outlined in this eBook, you are well-equipped to launch and manage effective review incentive programs that drive long-term business growth.

Good luck, and may your journey to gathering positive reviews be rewarding and successful!

Resources

To successfully implement and manage your review incentive programs, leveraging the right tools and platforms is crucial. Here are two highly recommended resources to help you streamline your efforts and achieve your goals:

HiVirtancy (https://hivirtancy.com)

HiVirtancy is an all-in-one platform that provides powerful CRM and automation tools to enhance your review incentive programs. Here's how HiVirtancy can support your efforts:

1. **Comprehensive CRM**:

    o **Customer Data Management**: HiVirtancy's CRM allows you to centralize and manage customer data efficiently. Track purchase history, review activity, and preferences to personalize your incentives.

    o **Segmentation**: Segment your customer base based on various criteria to target your review incentives more precisely.

2. **Automation Tools**:

    o **Automated Campaigns**: Set up automated email campaigns to request reviews, send reminders, and deliver rewards. Customize the timing and content to match customer behavior and preferences.

- **Triggered Responses**: Use automation to trigger responses based on customer actions. Send thank-you emails, discount codes, and loyalty points automatically after a review is submitted.

3. **Loyalty Program Integration**:

- **Points Tracking**: HiVirtancy integrates seamlessly with your loyalty program, automatically tracking points earned from reviews and ensuring accuracy.

- **Reward Redemption**: Simplify the process of reward redemption by linking it to your CRM. Notify customers when they earn enough points and provide clear instructions for redeeming rewards.

4. **Analytics and Reporting**:

- **Performance Metrics**: Track key performance indicators (KPIs) such as the number of reviews, review quality, and customer engagement. Use this data to measure the effectiveness of your incentive programs.

- **Data-Driven Insights**: Analyze customer feedback and behavior to refine your strategies and continuously improve your review incentives.

TrustTrendy (https://TrustTrendy.com)

TrustTrendy is an all-in-one review management platform designed to help businesses collect, manage, and display customer reviews effectively. Here's how TrustTrendy can enhance your review incentive programs:

1. **Review Collection**:

   o **Streamlined Process**: TrustTrendy simplifies the process of collecting reviews from customers. Use customizable review request templates and automated follow-ups to increase review submissions.

   o **Multi-Channel Collection**: Collect reviews from various channels, including email, social media, and your website, ensuring you capture feedback from a wide audience.

2. **Review Management**:

   o **Centralized Dashboard**: Manage all your reviews from a single, user-friendly dashboard. Monitor review activity, respond to feedback, and address customer concerns promptly.

   o **Moderation Tools**: Use advanced moderation tools to filter and manage reviews, ensuring that only genuine and relevant feedback is displayed.

3. **Display and Promotion**:

- **Customizable Widgets**: Showcase customer reviews on your website using customizable widgets. Enhance your site's credibility and influence potential customers with positive feedback.

- **Social Proof**: Leverage positive reviews in your marketing campaigns to build trust and attract new customers. Share reviews on social media and include them in email newsletters.

4. **Analytics and Insights**:

- **Review Analytics**: Analyze review trends, sentiment, and customer feedback to gain valuable insights. Use this data to improve your products, services, and customer experience.

- **Performance Reports**: Generate detailed performance reports to track the impact of your review incentive programs. Identify areas for improvement and optimize your strategies.

By utilizing HiVirtancy and TrustTrendy, you can effectively manage and enhance your review incentive programs, driving more positive reviews and building a loyal customer base. These platforms provide the tools and insights needed to streamline your efforts and achieve long-term success.

www.ingramcontent.com/pod-product-compliance
Lightning Source LLC
Chambersburg PA
CBHW071951210526
45479CB00003B/899